OWEN DAVEY

WILD ABOUT WHALES

FLYING EYE BOOKS

Rice's whale

CONTENTS

6   What are Whales?

8   By Design

10   Whale Watching

12   A Fluke of Nature

14   Give Us a Call

16   Born This Way

18   Making a Meal of Things

20   Wolves of the Sea

22   Little and Large

24   To Scale

26   And the Award Goes To...

28   Weird and Wonderful

30   Whale of a Time

32   Whale Mythology

34   Conservation

36   Index

WHAT ARE WHALES?

Whales are mammals that spend their whole lives in water. They are not fish, and cannot breathe underwater. In fact, their closest relative is actually the hippopotamus! Scientifically, whales are called cetaceans, pronounced set-ay-shns.

Whales are divided into two suborders. Depending on which marine biologist you ask, there are around 77 toothed whales and 15 baleen whales. Toothed whales, including dolphins and porpoises, use their teeth to hunt, while baleen whales filter food from the sea using special baleen plates in their mouths.

Common dolphin

Common minke whale

Habitat

Most whales live in the open ocean, but a few toothed whale species are adapted for life in freshwater rivers. Most whales migrate each year, travelling long distances to find food-rich parts of the ocean or warm waters for their young.

Nom Nom

All whales are carnivores. Baleen whales are among the largest animals in the world, but tend to have a diet of tiny organisms like krill and zooplankton as well as small crustaceans and fish. Toothed whales hunt a wide range of food, including fish, squid, seals, octopuses, penguins, sharks, eels, rays, and even other species of whale!

Pacific white-sided dolphin

Great Whales

Baleen whales are huge creatures and are often called the 'great whales'. Even the smallest species – the pygmy right whale – is about six and a half metres (21 ft) long! Baleen whales tend to live alone or form small temporary groups, while toothed whales usually live in pods and are very social.

BY DESIGN

To better understand these remarkable creatures, take a closer look at the baleen and toothed whales below.

Eyes

A shiny layer at the back of their eyes called the 'tapetum lucidum' helps whales to see in dark or murky water.

Tongue

Baleen whale tongues help push water out through the baleen plates, leaving prey behind to swallow.

Blubber

Whales are covered in this thick layer of fat to help them float, keep warm, and store energy.

Blowhole

A blowhole is a nostril, but unlike us, whales have their nostrils on the top of their heads. Baleen whales have two blowholes while toothed whales have only one. When they go underwater, a 'nasal plug' seals the blowhole so water can't get in.

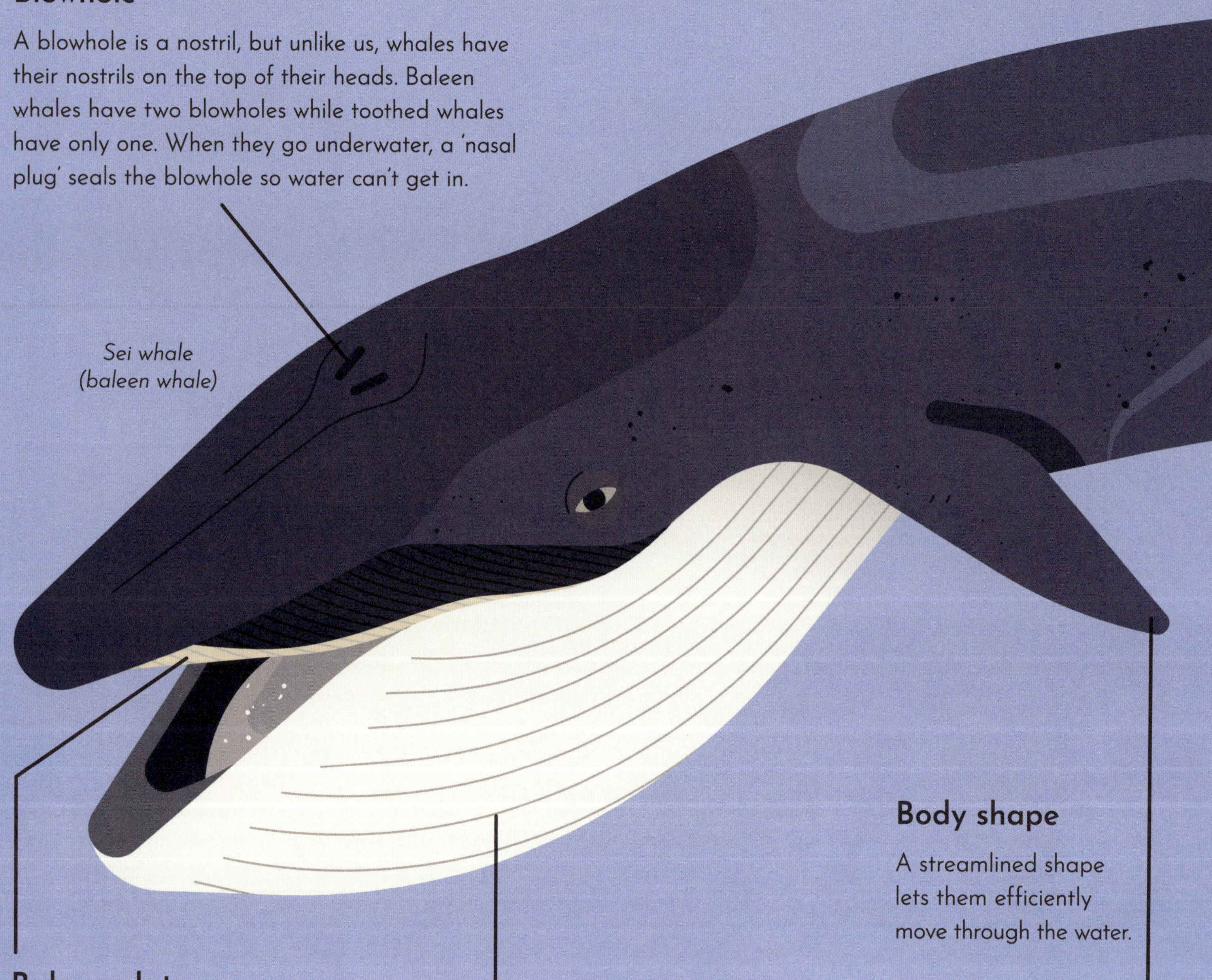

Body shape

A streamlined shape lets them efficiently move through the water.

Baleen plates

Baleen whales have comb-like baleen plates instead of teeth. They are made of keratin similar to our fingernails, and work like a sieve, filtering out water and trapping prey.

Ventral pleats

Folds of skin, pleated like in a skirt, allowing it to grow and shrink to take in large amounts of water and food.

Pectoral fin

Also known as flippers, these help with balance, steering, and turning in the water.

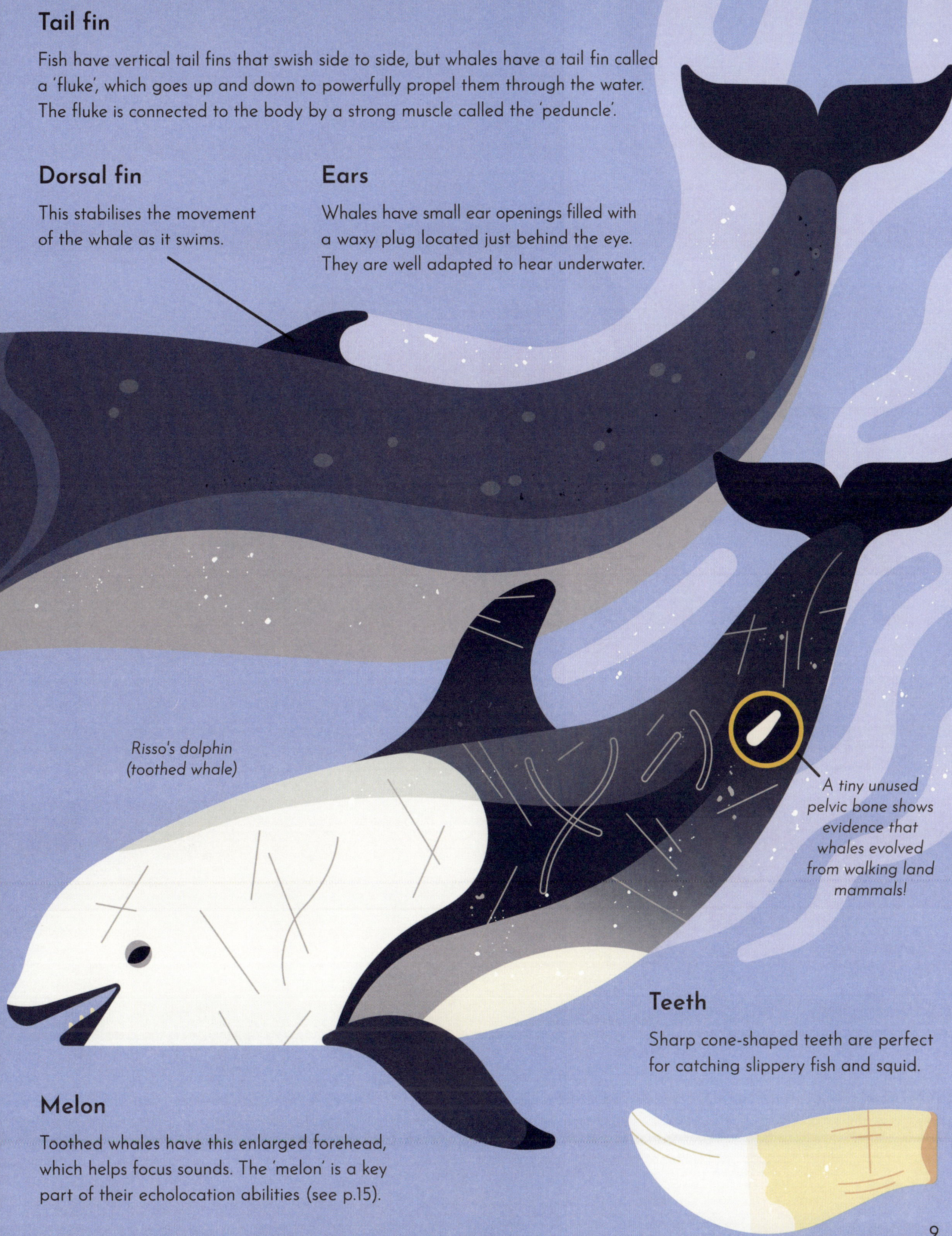

Tail fin

Fish have vertical tail fins that swish side to side, but whales have a tail fin called a 'fluke', which goes up and down to powerfully propel them through the water. The fluke is connected to the body by a strong muscle called the 'peduncle'.

Dorsal fin

This stabilises the movement of the whale as it swims.

Ears

Whales have small ear openings filled with a waxy plug located just behind the eye. They are well adapted to hear underwater.

Teeth

Sharp cone-shaped teeth are perfect for catching slippery fish and squid.

Melon

Toothed whales have this enlarged forehead, which helps focus sounds. The 'melon' is a key part of their echolocation abilities (see p.15).

WHALE WATCHING

Eventually, whales have to come to the surface of the water to breathe. Some species can hold their breath for a few hours, while others can only last a few minutes. Naturally, this is the easiest time for humans to find and watch whales.

Breached Whale

Whales can leap out of the water (called a 'breach'). The size and power of this display is one of the most spectacular sights in the natural world, but we don't fully understand why they do it. The loud splash caused by the activity can be heard from miles away, so many scientists believe that one reason whales breach is to communicate with other whales.

Humpback whale

Some species, especially the humpback whale, roll onto their sides and slap the water with their pectoral fins.

Southern right whale

Whales may raise their flukes above the water before a deep dive. On some occasions, they may also slap the water with their tails, known as 'lobtailing', which could be a sign of communication.

Orca

Whales sometimes poke their head above the water to get a glimpse of their surroundings. This is known as 'spy-hopping'.

Here's My Spout

When a whale surfaces, its breath can look like a spray of water, known as a 'spout' or 'blow'. Spouts are the warm air from their lungs mixing with the cold air outside and condensing into a cloud - exactly like your breath does on a cold day. The shape of the spout can often help us identify the species of whale it belongs to - a blue whale's spout can be more than 10 metres (32.8 ft) tall!

This spout may also have some seawater droplets in it and a little bit of whale snot... yuck!

What's the Porpoise?

Whales have powerful flukes to propel them through the water but many toothed whales can swim so fast that they go airborne. This well-known dolphin movement, known as 'porpoising', lets these whales jump through the air, which has much less resistance than water. It requires less effort, keeps them moving fast, and allows them to breathe without having to slow down.

A FLUKE OF NATURE

Featured Creatures: Humpback Whales

One of the most popular whales to see on whale watching tours is the humpback whale. They spend much of their winters near coastlines where their powerful breaches, dramatic fin slaps, complex calls, and impressive flukes are regularly on display.

The distinctive bumps on the head and fins of humpback whales are called 'tubercles'. Each one contains a hair follicle with a single stiff hair.

Along with blue whales, humpbacks have the longest pectoral fins in the whale kingdom, reaching five metres (16 ft) and nearly a third of the length of their bodies.

Home from Home

Whale migration is an essential part of life for many whale species. Polar regions often have an abundance of nutrient-rich food in summer, such as krill, but the cold waters eventually force them to retreat back to warmer regions in winter. Some eat almost exclusively in the summer months, consuming around 1.5 tonnes of food a day. For more than half the year, they don't eat anything at all.

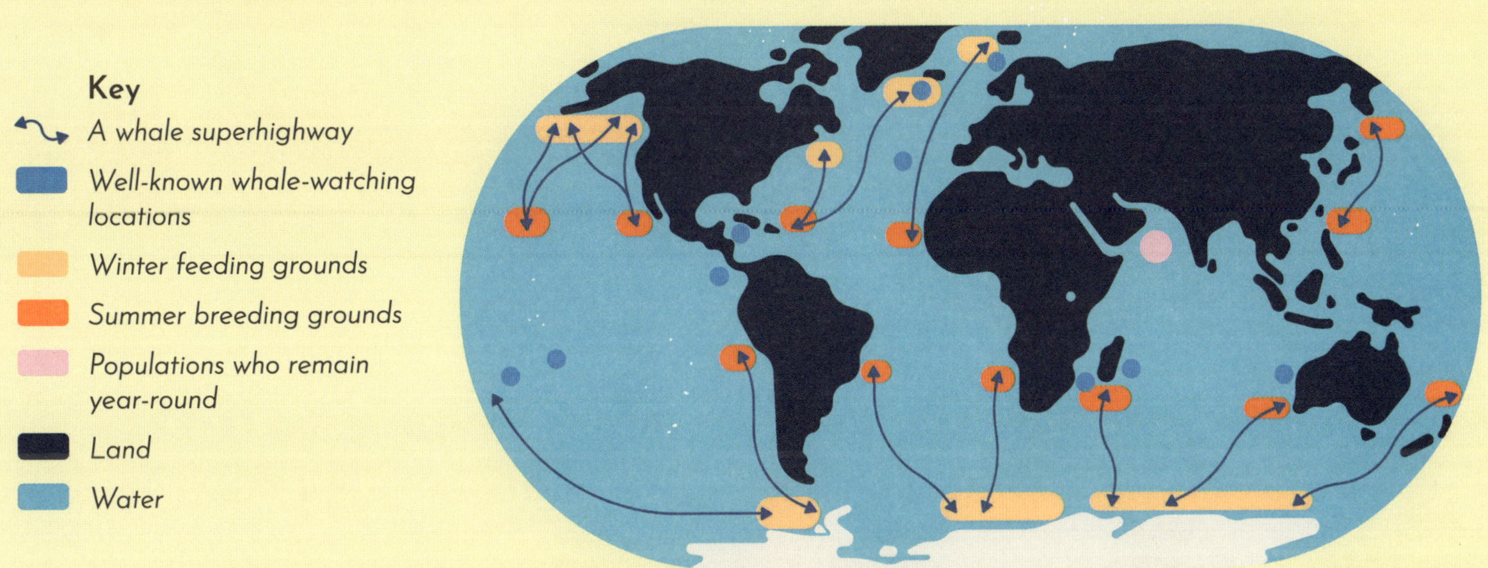

The most popular whale migration routes are called 'whale superhighways'. The humpback whale can migrate for thousands of miles, sometimes up to or over a 10,000 mile (16,093 km) round-trip! This migration is one of the longest in the animal kingdom. This map shows how they navigate the world.

GIVE US A CALL

Whales mainly communicate with sound. They can click, whistle, coo, grunt, groan, snort, bark, and even sing complex songs.

Low and Slow

Low-frequency (deep) sounds travel much further in water than in air and move around four times quicker too. Noises made near the surface can bounce off the water's edge and quickly disappear, so the best way for a whale to get themselves heard is to dive deep first. The loudest animals in the world are the whales: the blue whale and sperm whale. Their slow and deep sounds are louder than a jet engine, and can be heard thousands of miles away.

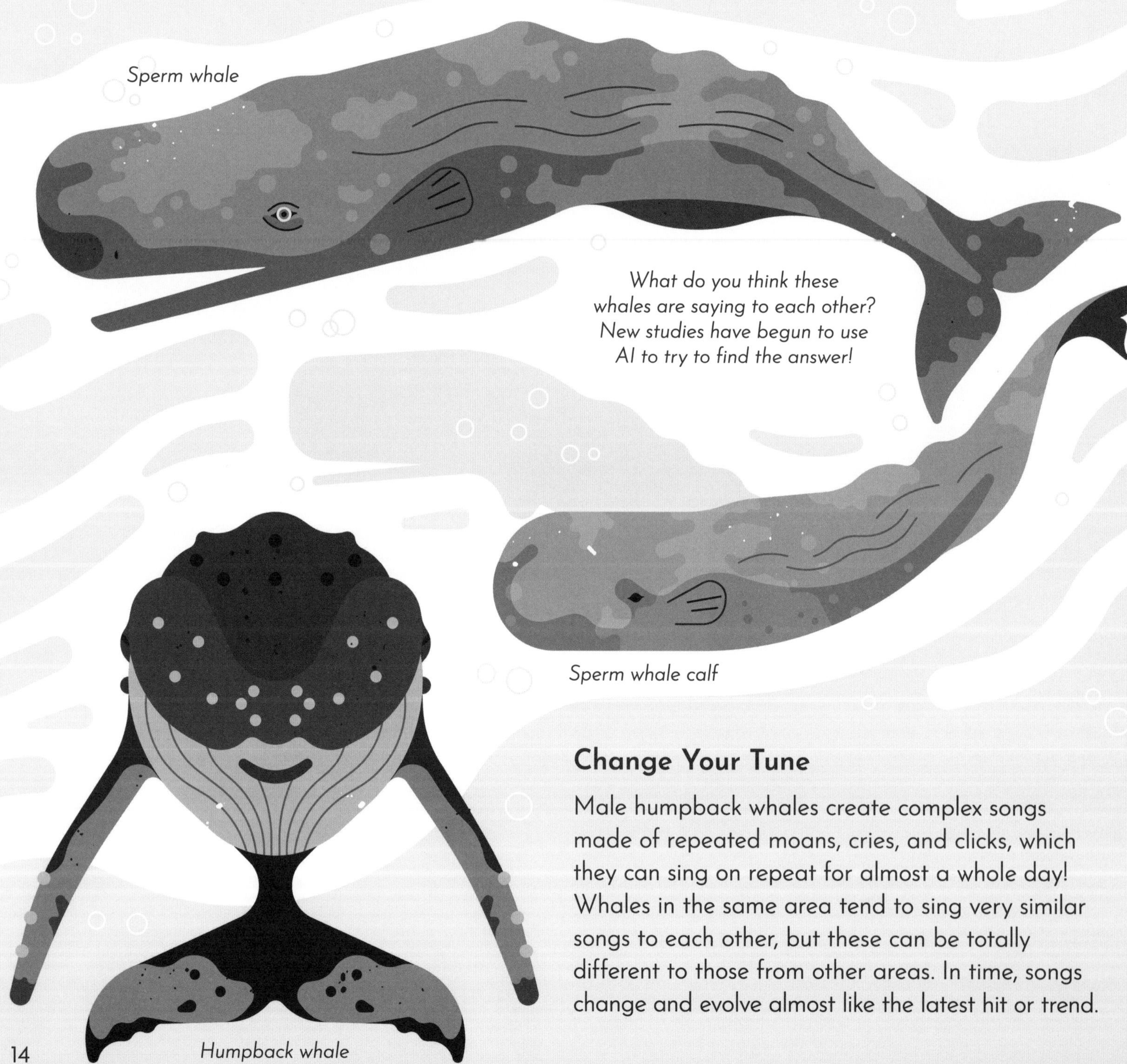

Sperm whale

Sperm whale calf

Humpback whale

Change Your Tune

Male humpback whales create complex songs made of repeated moans, cries, and clicks, which they can sing on repeat for almost a whole day! Whales in the same area tend to sing very similar songs to each other, but these can be totally different to those from other areas. In time, songs change and evolve almost like the latest hit or trend.

14

Echo... Echo... Echo

Toothed whales use echolocation to map their surroundings using sound. They use their melon to focus narrow beams of sound in a certain direction. This rebounds off whatever is there before returning back to them as an echo. This method is so precise that they can not only locate their prey, but figure out its size, movement, and even what type of animal it is.

No human technology can replicate the advanced echolocation of bottlenose dolphins. Controversially, in some countries (like the USA), the navy has used them to detect unexploded mines with remarkable accuracy.

Bottlenose dolphin

Beluga whale

When Life Gives You Melons...

Beluga whales are known as the canaries of the sea because they produce a wide range of sounds, from clicks and squeals to buzzes and roars. Their large flexible melon changes shape and even wobbles to help navigate the icy environments they live in.

BORN THIS WAY

Whales produce live young, which are born
tail-first into the water. They must then come
up to the surface to breathe for the first time,
often helped by their mother or her relatives.

*The frilly tongue of a
bottlenose dolphin calf.*

Cows and Calves

Female whales are called cows, males are bulls,
and their babies are called calves. The calves drink
milk from their mothers, just like cows on land.
Some calf tongues have frilly edges that form a
watertight seal while they drink, to stop them from
gulping water instead. Whale milk is extremely fatty
and helps the calves grow quickly. In fact, blue whale
calves gain up to 100kg (220 lb) of weight each
day – that's one tonne in 10 days!

Mother and Baby

Calves stay close to their mothers for six months to a year. They even get carried along by staying in her slip stream to make it much easier to swim. This is known as 'echelon swimming' and helps form a bond between them, protects the calf from potential predators, like orcas, and makes it easier for milk feeding. In some species, whales join the pod and remain with their mother their whole lives.

Baby Talk

Many dolphins speak to their calves with a higher pitch than they do to other dolphins, similar to the way human parents will speak to their babies. Mother and calf humpback whales also 'whisper' to each other to communicate without alerting predators.

MAKING A MEAL OF THINGS

Baleen whales are filter feeders, swallowing big mouthfuls of water containing their prey and then forcing the water through their baleen, leaving only the meal to swallow. These large predators need a lot of energy from their food, so they must consume huge quantities of their small prey to survive. Toothed whales use their teeth to catch and eat fish, squid, or seals, or swallow small prey whole.

In For the Krill

Krill are a major food source of many baleen whales. They are shrimp-like creatures that live in dense swarms of up to 10,000 individuals per cubic metre. These swarms can be anything from a few metres wide, to several miles long! Some whales may eat up to 30% of their own body weight in krill a day. Blue whales can eat four tonnes of krill daily, and they can make up 90 per cent of its diet.

Humpback whale

What a Big Mouth You Have

A group of whales known as the rorquals, are the largest species of baleen whales. Rorquals lunge feed by quickly propelling themselves towards a school of fish or krill with their mouth wide open.

North Atlantic right whale

Go Slow

Right whales and bowhead whales skim feed by swimming slowly at the surface with their mouths open like a sieve to filter their food.

Grey whale

Stir Things Up

Grey whales are bottom-feeders (don't laugh). They swim sideways and roll to stir up sediment along the ocean floor. This 'mud-ploughing' reveals creatures hidden within it, which are filtered through their baleen.

Humpback whale

You Herd Me

Whales create bubbles when they release air underwater, just like us. Humpbacks use this to their advantage in a technique known as 'bubble-net feeding'. They swim in circles below a school of fish and blow bubbles through their blowholes, which creates a sort of net, trapping the fish and forcing them to group together so the whales can catch more fish when they lunge.

Blainville's beaked whale

Whales Suck

Toothed beaked whales are suction feeders, having lost most of their functional teeth. During deep dives, they adjust their lungs to avoid pressure damage and create a low-pressure environment in their mouths. To catch fast and agile prey like squid, they open their mouths quickly, causing high-pressure water, and prey, to rush in.

WOLVES OF THE SEA

Featured Creatures: Orca

Like most toothed whales, orcas live in family groups called 'pods'. Also known as killer whales, they are efficient and strategic predators who work together to catch prey. Orcas are the largest of all dolphin species, with teeth as long and sharp as a lion's. They hunt everything from penguins and seals to minke whales and even great white sharks!

Populations

Orcas can be found in all our oceans. Even within subspecies of orca, different populations have different regional accents, cultures, diets, and hunting tactics!

The orcas that live along the West coast of North America have been studied by scientists for decades. There are three distinct subspecies in this area:

Resident orcas mostly eat fish, and are particularly fond of salmon. These orcas have strong bonds with each other and stay in matrilineal pods, meaning all the orcas are directly related to one female ancestor.

Transient orcas specialise in hunting marine mammals like dolphins and seals. Like all orcas they can communicate with many different noises, but during a hunt these orcas go silent to stay stealthy.

Offshore orcas live in large groups of more than 50 individuals. They tend to spend most of their time in deeper water away from land and they eat fish, specialising in hunting sharks.

Here are some ingenious hunting tactics that orcas use:

Feeling Stranded

In shallow coastal waters, prey is chased onto beaches. Transient orcas temporarily beach themselves to retrieve the target, then return to the water.

All Comes Out in the Wash

Some orcas spy hop to locate seals on ice, then work together to dislodge them. The orcas may knock the ice with their bodies or work together to create waves that wash the seal into the water.

On the Ball

Working together, resident orcas herd salmon into tight balls known as a 'bait ball'. Members of the pod then take it in turns to slap the bait ball with their tail to stun the fish.

Stunning Technique

Offshore orcas ram great white sharks to flip them onto their backs. This stuns the sharks and puts them into a relaxed unmoving state known as 'tonic immobility'. The orcas then eat the nutrient-rich liver, leaving the rest of the carcass to other animals.

LITTLE AND LARGE

Featured Creatures: Blue Whales

Blue whales are thought to be the largest animal
to have ever lived! The longest blue whales can be
more than 30 metres (98 ft) long - the same as three
buses lined up one behind the other. A blue whale can
hold 80,000 litres of water in its mouth from a single
gulp - about the same as a swimming pool.

Featured Creatures: Vaquita

Vaquita are the smallest species of whale at only around 1.5 metres (4.9 ft) in length. They have a distinctive dark circle around their eyes. They are the most endangered marine animal in the world – it is thought that there are fewer than 10 of these porpoises left. Their population decline is largely due to the use of meshed fishing nets that are very efficient at catching fish, but can also catch whales, sea turtles, and seals by accident, known as 'bycatch'. Vaquita have the smallest range of any cetacean, just off the coast of Mexico, and the use of these fishing nets in this area has been banned since 2017.

TO SCALE
This scuba diver is 1.7 meters (5.5 ft) tall. Compare their size to these whales,
ranging from the smallest (vaquita) to largest (blue whale) species.
grey whale
narwhal
minke whale
Baird's beaked whale
bottlenose dolphin
vaquita
humpback whale
Blainville's beaked whale
5 metres
20 feet

southern right whale
beluga whale
harbour porpoise
orca
blue whale
spinner dolphin
sperm whale
long-finned pilot whale
fin whale

AND THE AWARD GOES TO...

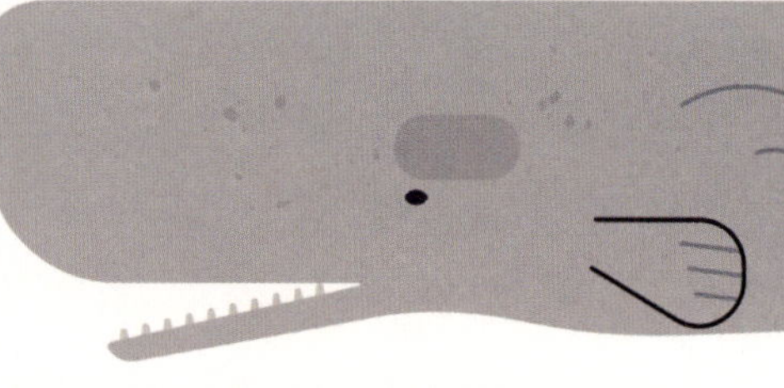

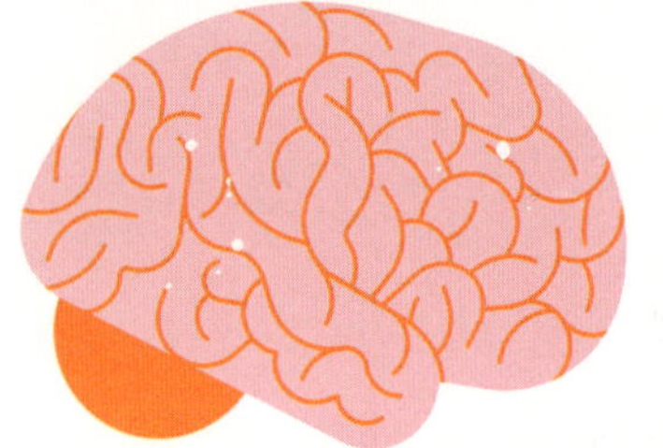

Human brain

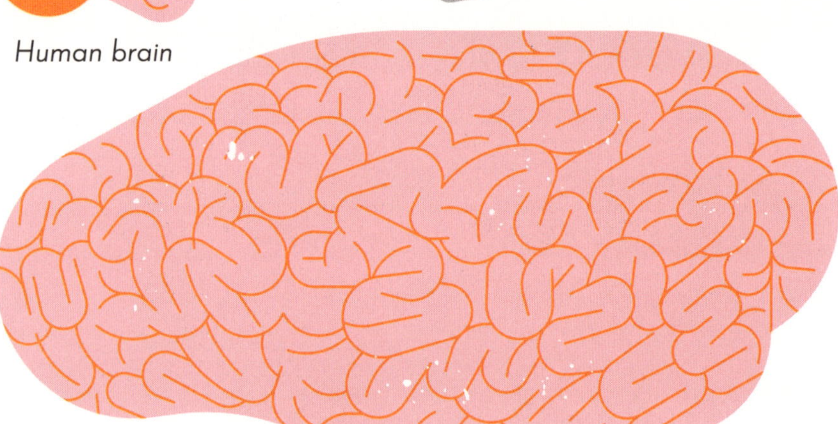

Sperm whale brain

Sperm whales have the largest brain of any animal species – it is five times larger than the human brain. Their huge box-shaped heads take up about 40% of their total body length, and their brains are nearly half a metre (1.6 ft) long.

Grey whale

Grey whales endure one of the longest migrations of any mammal. Their round trip from Mexico to the Arctic can take nearly half a year, covering nearly 14,000 miles (22,530 km)!

Bowhead whale earwax

Bowhead whale

Bowhead whales win the award for the longest lifespan. By counting the layers of earwax on a whale's ear plug, we can estimate a whale's age, much like counting the rings on a tree. Most whales live between 30 and 100 years, but some bowhead whales can live for more than 200 years!

Orcas are the fastest whales in our oceans. Their usual swimming speed is only around 2-5 mph, close to a human's walking speed, but they can reach almost 35 mph. An orca pod can cover more than 100 miles (160 km) in a day.

The awards for deepest and longest dives by any mammal are claimed by the Cuvier's beaked whale. These toothed whales have been recorded diving nearly 1.8 miles (3 km) deep and lasting more than 2 hours between breaths.

WEIRD AND WONDERFUL

The grey whale is infested with barnacles and small crustacean parasites called 'whale lice', which feed on their skin.

Beluga whales are born dark grey, but turn white by the time they're eight years old. They live among icy waters and have a thick layer of blubber to keep them warm.

Pink river dolphins feed on fish, turtles, and crabs in the waters of the Amazon and Orinoco rivers in South America. They are born grey, but become more pink with age.

Right whales are distinctive for their rounded
shape, grumpy-looking mouths and the calluses
on their heads, which are rough patches of skin.
These calluses are unique to each right whale.

Narwhals are often called the unicorns of the sea
because of their iconic spiral tusk, which is actually
an enlarged tooth that grows through their forehead.

Male strap-toothed whales grow tusks from their lower
jaws, which extend over their snouts and sometimes
overlap at the ends. This can reduce how wide
they can open their mouths! Each tusk has
a small, sharp 'denticle' poking out at
the tip, used for fighting.

WHALE OF A TIME

Featured Creatures: Bottlenose Dolphins

Playtime

Bottlenose dolphins love to play. They are known to play both catch and tag and also love to surf. Some whale species surf waves exclusively to save energy, but dolphins often do it just for fun. They ride waves at the beach alongside human surfers, and even play in the wakes of boats.

A group of young males spend time in the waves.

My Name Is...

Did you know that bottlenose dolphins have names? They're not names like you and I would have, but every dolphin has a signature whistle that is unique to them. They will introduce themselves to other dolphins this way, and some individuals have even been heard mimicking the signature whistle of another individual to get their attention.

"Look at me!"

A Sense of Self

Bottlenose dolphins can recognise themselves in a mirror. If paint is temporarily applied to their bodies, they try to investigate or remove the marks, realising that they are looking at their own reflection. While this might seem simple to us, animals like dogs and cats typically fail this mirror test, mistaking their reflection for another animal.

Pass It On

Whales have the amazing ability to teach each other things, often from mother to child. They can teach songs and sounds, hunting techniques and safe migration routes. Some female bottlenose dolphins in Australia have discovered how to use marine sponges to protect their snouts while foraging for food on the rough sea floor. Amazingly, this knowledge will now be passed - to their daughters, but not their sons - for generations to come.

Pod Help Us

There are countless tales of dolphins coming to the aid of humans and other creatures by guiding them to safety or bringing help. There are even stories of them nudging drowning humans back onto boats to save them. Heroic stories like these have been told for more than 300 years. It is hard to know exactly why dolphins do this, but many believe it is simply to help others.

WHALE MYTHOLOGY

Unicorn Horn

In medieval Europe, belief in unicorns was widespread. Until the 1700s, wealthy and powerful people bought 'unicorn horns', thinking they were magical. Small pieces of those horns were added to their drinks, believed to protect them from harm. Queen Elizabeth I famously drank from a golden goblet said to be carved from a 'unicorn horn', trusting it would purify water. In reality, these unicorn horns were the iconic tusks of the narwhal.

Cá Ông

In Vietnam, whales are revered as the gods of the Southern Sea, known as Cá Ông, which roughly translates to 'Lord Whale.' Fishermen pray to Cá Ông before heading out to sea, seeking success in their catch and protection from danger. Many fishermen recount first-hand experiences of whales guiding them back to shore during storms or coming to their aid in perilous situations. If a whale is found dead, it is considered a sacred duty to bring it ashore, conduct a proper burial, and mourn it as you would a beloved family member.

Jonah and the Whale

In the Bible, when Jonah was thrown from his ship during a storm, a giant sea creature swallowed him whole, saving his life. He lived inside the creature for three days and nights before being safely released onto the shore. In Christianity, this animal is often depicted as a great whale, but in the original Hebrew text, it is described as a 'big fish'.

Bake-kujira

The 'bone whale' is a Japanese yōkai (ghost). This huge baleen whale skeleton swims in the ocean followed by huge schools of fish and strange birds.

CONSERVATION

Baleen whale species were hunted nearly to extinction before commercial whaling bans were put into effect. Thankfully, many whale populations have rebounded well. Humpback whales, for instance, have nearly returned to their pre-whaling numbers. However, whales today face significant threats, including overfishing, bycatch, pollution, climate change, noise pollution, habitat destruction, and being struck by boats.

Eco Warriors

Why is protecting whales so important? Apart from their incredible intelligence, whales can empathise, cooperate, and even mourn their dead. Whales help combat climate change – their large bodies store significant amounts of carbon, and when they die, their bodies trap it on the ocean floor. Even their poo is important! It nourishes phytoplankton, tiny marine algae that absorb massive amounts of carbon and produce over half the oxygen in our atmosphere. By restoring whale populations, we could make a meaningful impact on climate change.

How Can I Help?

You can educate yourself by doing things like borrowing books about whales from the library, and researching whale conservation organisations online with your caregivers. When you're out shopping or eating, you and your friends and family can look out for the MSC label. It is a little blue badge with a white fish on it, and it stands for Marine Stewardship Council, which means the fish was caught in a way that keeps the ocean healthy and protects sea creatures. Don't be shy about being vocal about what you learn. Share your fascinating facts with others so that they can get involved too!

By protecting whales, we're not just safeguarding an iconic group of animals – we're helping maintain the health and future of our planet.

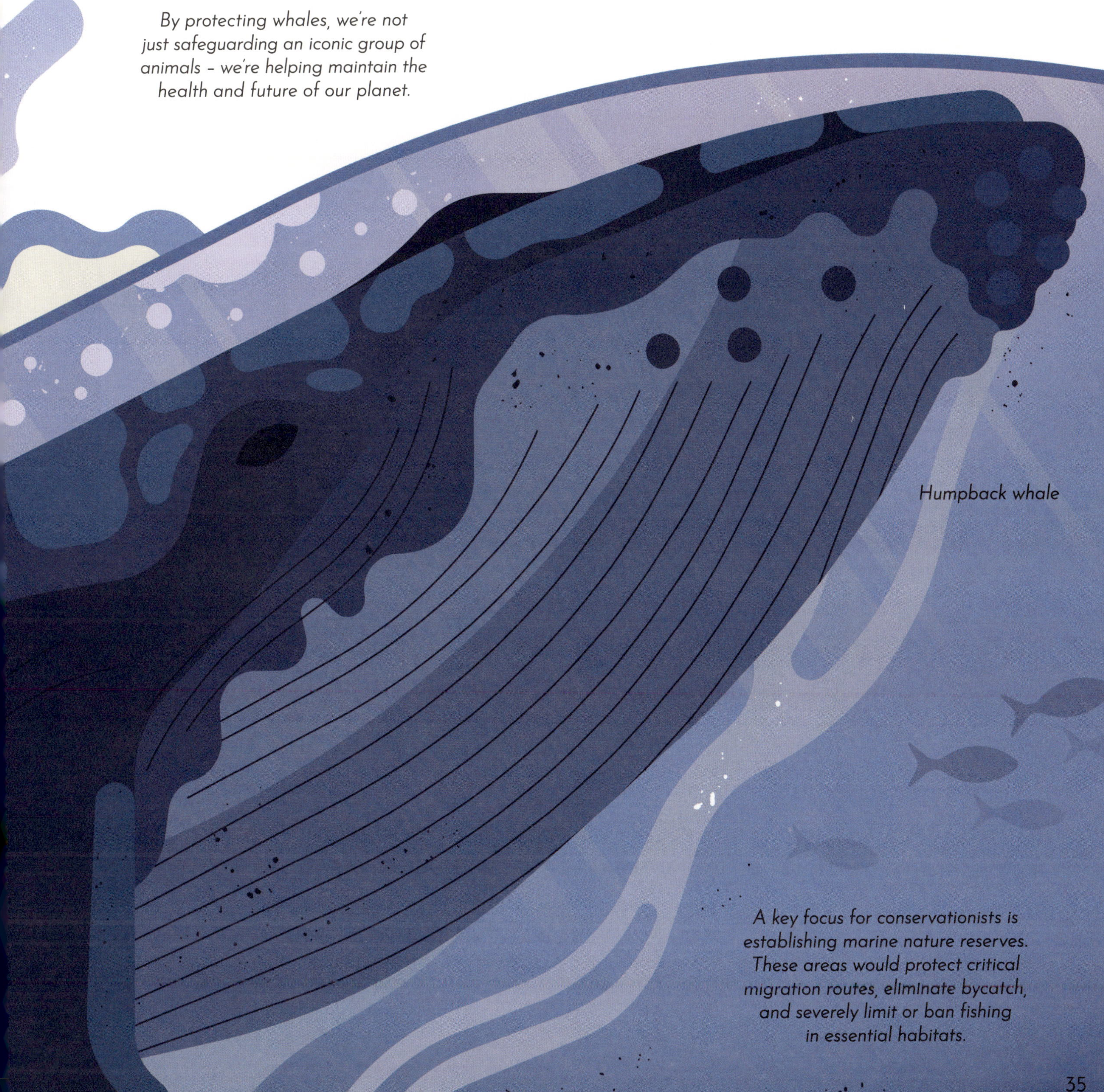

Humpback whale

A key focus for conservationists is establishing marine nature reserves. These areas would protect critical migration routes, eliminate bycatch, and severely limit or ban fishing in essential habitats.

INDEX

Toothed whales

Baird's beaked whale (Berardius bairdii) 24

Beluga (Delphinapterus leucas) 15, 25, 28

Blainville's beaked whale (Mesoplodon densirostris) 19,24

Bottlenose dolphin (Tursiops truncatus) 15-6, 24, 30-1

Commerson's dolphin (Cephalorhynchus commersonii) 16

Common dolphin (Delphinus delphis) 6

Cuvier's beaked whale (Ziphius cavirostris) 27

Dusky dolphin (Lagenorhynchus obscurus) 36

Harbour porpoise (Phocoena phocoena) 11, 25

Long-finned pilot whale (Globicephala melas) 25

Narwhal (Monodon monoceros) 24, 32

Pacific white-sided dolphin (Aethalodelphis obliquidens) 7

Pink river dolphin, Amazon river dolphin, boto (Inia geoffrensis) 28

Risso's dolphin (Grampus griseus) 9

Sperm whale (Physeter macrocephalus) 11, 14, 24-6

Spinner dolphin (Stenella longirostris) 25

Strap-toothed whale (Mesoplodon layardii) 29

Vaquita (Phocoena sinus) 23-4

Baleen whales

Blue whale (Balaenoptera musculus) 17, 22–4

Bowhead whale (Balaena mysticetus) 19, 26

Common minke whale (Balaenoptera acutorostrata) 6, 20, 24

Dall's porpoise (Phocoenoides dalli) 11

Fin whale (Balaenoptera physalus) 24–5

Grey whale (Eschrichtius robustus) 19, 24, 26, 28

Humpback whale (Megaptera novaeangliae) 11–4, 19, 24, 34–5

North Atlantic right whale (Eubalaena glacialis) 19, 29

Orca (Orcinus orca) 10–1, 17, 20–1, 25, 27

Rice's whale (Balaenoptera ricei) 4

Sei whale (Balaenoptera borealis) 8,9

Southern right whale (Eubalaena australis) 11, 25

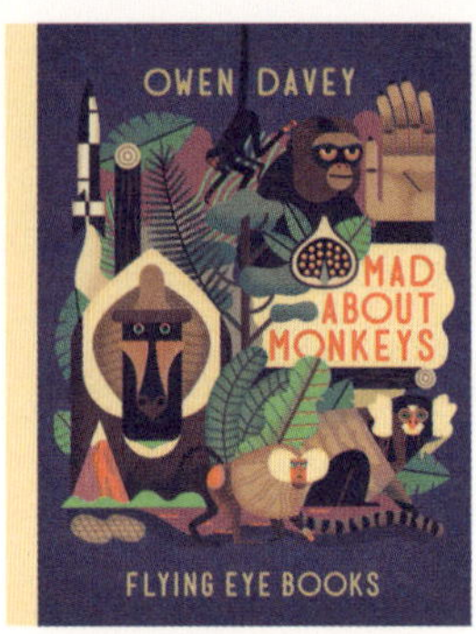

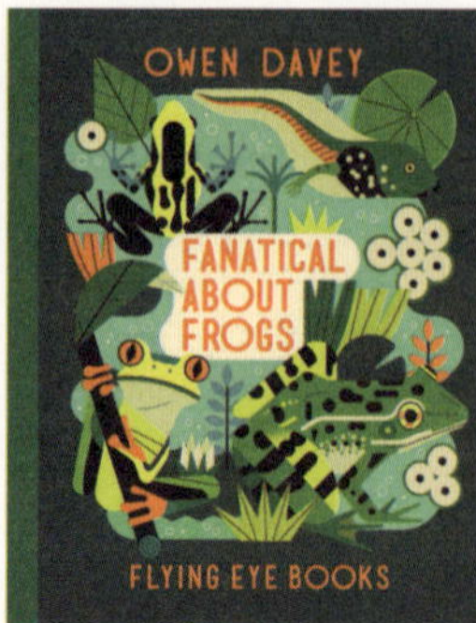
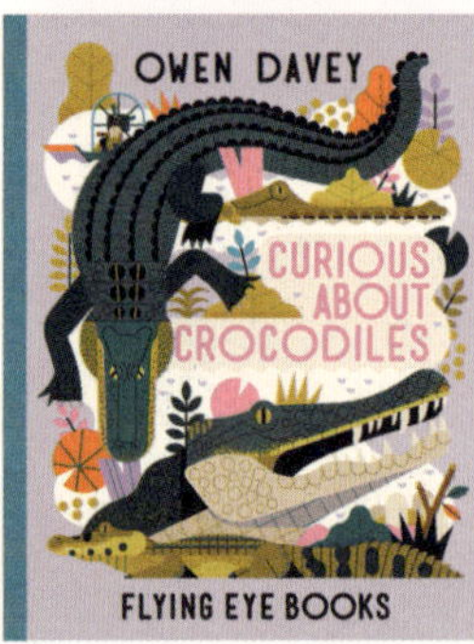
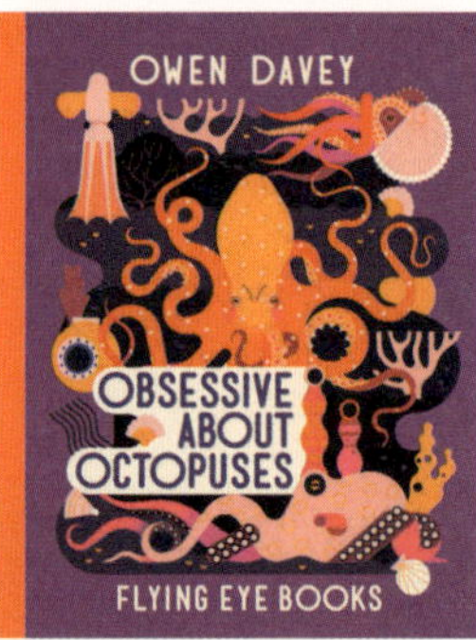

For Max, Henry, Oliver, William, Isabel, Alyssia, Albie, and Ellie.

Published in 2026 by Flying Eye Books Ltd.
27 Westgate Street, London, E8 3RL.
www.flyingeyebooks.com

Represented by: Abrams & Chronicle Books c/o Media Participations
57 rue Gaston Tessier, CS 50061
75166 Paris Cedex 19, France

www.media-participations.com/en/subsidiaries
productsafety@abramsandchronicle.co.uk

Text and illustrations © Owen Davey 2026

Edited by Fay Evans
Designed by Maisy Ruffels
Scientific consultant: Andy Rogan

1 3 5 7 9 10 8 6 4 2

ISBN: 978-1-83874-230-0

Printed in China on FSC® certified paper.